Sort It by SOUND

By Nicholas O'Hara

first concepts

Gareth Stevens
PUBLISHING

Sorting means putting things that are alike together. You can sort by sound.

Some things are loud.

Some things are quiet. Let's sort loud and quiet things.

Babies can be loud
or quiet.

Crying babies
are loud.

Puppies can be loud
or quiet.

Sleeping puppies
are quiet.

Weather can be
loud or quiet.

Snow is quiet.

Cars and trucks
can be loud or quiet.

A fire truck
can be loud.

Water can be loud
or quiet.

Big waves are loud.

Birds can be loud
or quiet.

Roosters can be loud.

People can be loud
or quiet.

Whispers are quiet.

Music can be loud
or quiet.

Drums can be loud.

Look at this park.
Which things do
you think are loud?
Which are quiet?

Please visit our website, www.garethstevens.com. For a free color catalog of all our high-quality books, call toll free 1-800-542-2595 or fax 1-877-542-2596.

Library of Congress Cataloging-in-Publication Data

O'Hara, Nicholas.
Sort It by sound / by Nicholas O'Hara.
p. cm. — (Sort it out!)
Includes index.
ISBN 978-1-4824-2577-2 (pbk.)
ISBN 978-1-4824-2578-9 (6 pack)
ISBN 978-1-4824-2579-6 (library binding)
1. Sound — Juvenile literature. I. O'Hara, Nicholas. II. Title.
QC225.5 .O43 2016
534'.078—d23

First Edition

Published in 2016 by
Gareth Stevens Publishing
111 East 14th Street, Suite 349
New York, NY 10003

Designer: Sarah Liddell
Editor: Therese Shea

Photo credits: Cover, p. 1 (polka dots) Victoria Kalinina/Shutterstock.com; cover, p. 1 (instruments) koi88/Shutterstock.com; p. 3 Sergey Novikov/Shutterstock.com; pp. 4, 8 (right) Eric Isselee/Shutterstock.com; p. 5 Tsekhmister/Shutterstock.com; p. 6 (left) Flashon Studio/Shutterstock.com; p. 6 (right) Dmytro Vietrov/Shutterstock.com; p. 7 Boumen Japet/Shutterstock.com; p. 8 (left) WilleeCole Photography/Shutterstock.com; p. 9 oksana2010/Shutterstock.com; p. 10 Nomad_Soul/Shutterstock.com; p. 11 LilKar/Shutterstock.com; p. 12 (left) Maksim Toome/Shutterstock.com; pp. 12 (right), 13 Rob Wilson/Shutterstock.com; p. 14 Ray Esteves/Shutterstock.com; p. 15 Andrey Yurlov/Shutterstock.com; p. 16 (chicken) Valentina_S/Shutterstock.com; p. 16 (chicks) Gelpi JM Shutterstock.com; p. 17 yevgeniy11/Shutterstock.com; p. 18 (couple) Andresr/Shutterstock.com; p. 18 (right man) Aaron Amat/Shutterstock.com; p. 19 Nanette Grebe/Shutterstock.com; p. 20 (left) Prezoom.nl/Shutterstock.com; p. 20 (right) Pete Pahham/Shutterstock.com; p. 21 Anton Havelaar/Shutterstock.com; p. 23 Panoramic Images/Getty Images.

Printed in the United States of America

CPSIA compliance information: Batch #CS15GS: For further information contact Gareth Stevens, New York, New York at 1-800-542-2595.